The Nature Kid's Guide to
COYOTES

DAVID ANDERSON

LP Media Inc. Publishing
Text copyright © 2026 by LP Media Inc.
All rights reserved.

For information address LP Media Inc. Publishing,
30012 Variolite St NW, Princeton MN 55371
www.lpmedia.org

Publication Data

Coyotes
The Nature Kid's Guide to Coyotes — First edition.

Summary: "Learn all about Coyotes, the Nature Kid Way"
— Provided by publisher.

ISBN: 979-8-89818-163-5

[1. Coyotes – Non-Fiction] I. Title.

Title: The Nature Kid's Guide to Coyotes

CONTENTS

Home Sweet Home 4

Coast to Coast 6

Sizing Up 8

Built to Survive 10

Super Sniffers 12

Clever Camo 14

Chow Time 16

Crafty Hunters 18

Watch Out 20

Quick Getaway 22

Fast Feet 24

Day and Night 26

Pack Life 28

Finding Love 30

Cute Pups 32

Caring Coyotes 34

Super Survivors 36

Spot a Coyote 38

COYOTE COUNTRY

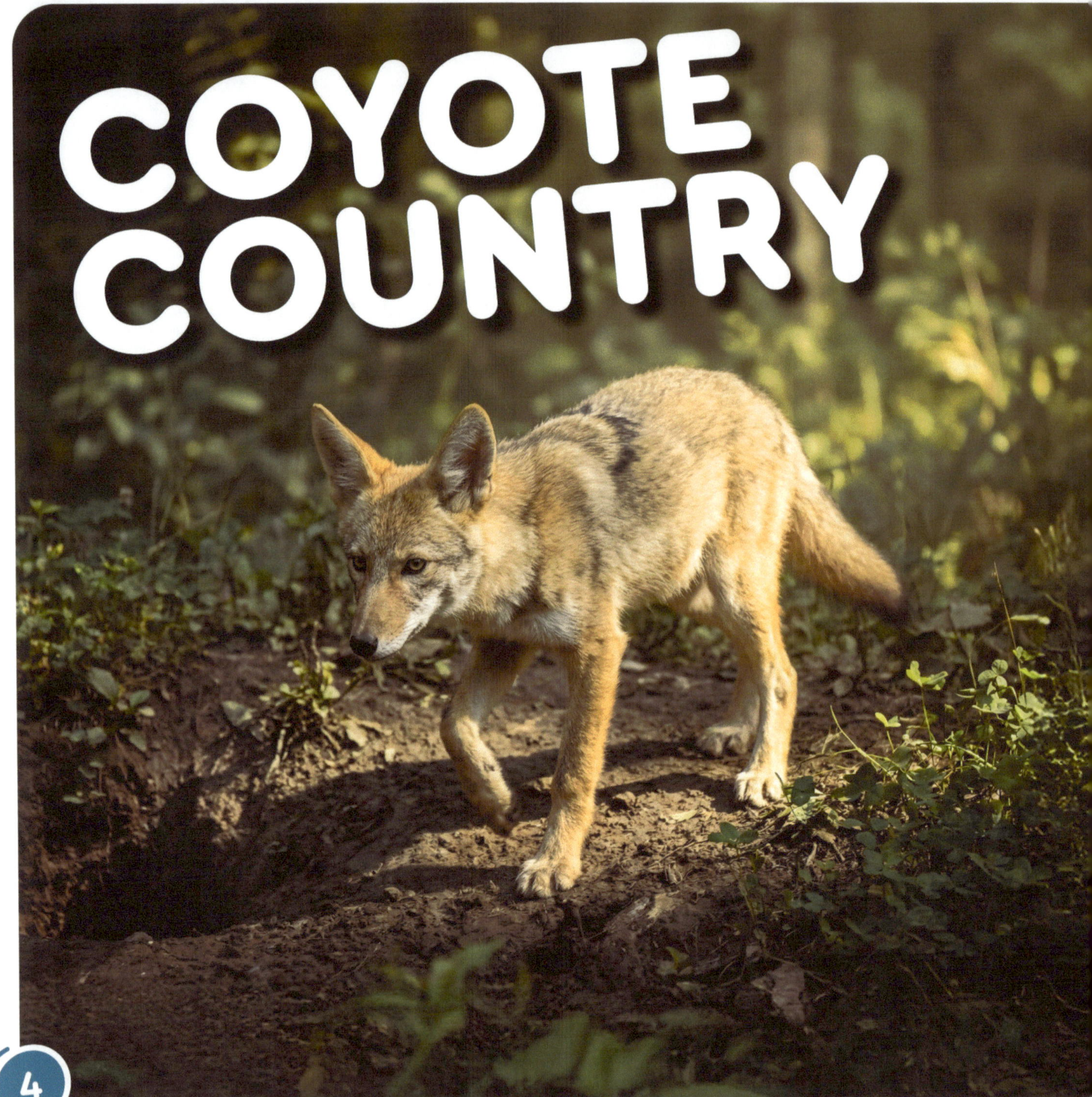

Crack! A twig breaks. A coyote trots to its den.

Coyotes live in many different habitats. They live in deserts. They live in forests. They live in grasslands. Some live near cities and towns.

Coyotes do well in hot weather. They do well in cold weather too. They can live in dry deserts. They can live on snowy mountains.

Coyotes like to hunt in open spaces. Prairies are good spots. They like tall grass and bushes. These spots help them hide and sneak up on their **prey**.

Coyotes and badgers hunt together! The badger digs underground. The coyote waits above to catch the prey that runs out.

COAST TO COAST

Spray! A coyote walks on a sandy beach. It sniffs the salty air.

Coyotes live across North America. They roam from Alaska to Panama. They live in Canada, the United States, and Mexico.

These animals spread to new places. They now live in all 49 states on the U.S. mainland. Only Hawaii has no wild coyotes.

Mountain coyotes live high up. Coastal coyotes live near beaches. City coyotes will even live in big cities like Los Angeles.

Coyotes reached New York City in 1995. Today they live in Central Park!

SIZING UP

Howl! The wind blows. A coyote trots across the open prairie.

Coyotes are medium-sized animals. They are as tall as a golden retriever. Most coyotes stand 21 to 26 inches at the shoulder.

A coyote weighs 20 to 50 pounds, about as much as a medium sized dog. But coyotes are much lighter than wolves.

Coyotes are 3 to 4 feet long from nose to tail. Their bushy tails add 12 to 16 more inches.

Male coyotes are bigger than females. They weigh about five pounds more on average.

BUILT TO SURVIVE

Coyotes can rotate each ear on its own to pinpoint sounds from far away!

Crack! A coyote steps on dry twigs in the brush. It freezes and listens.

Coyotes have bodies made for survival. Their thick fur keeps them warm in winter. It also protects them from hot summer sun.

Sharp teeth help coyotes eat many foods. Their long **canine** teeth grab prey. Back teeth crush bones and tough plants.

Strong legs and padded paws help coyotes move and hunt. Their claws dig **dens** and grip the ground.

Big pointed ears turn to catch sounds. Their yellow eyes also help them sense danger in dim light.

SUPER
SNIFFERS

Snort! The coyote breathes in scents from the wind.

Coyotes have amazing senses. Their noses can smell prey hiding underground. They can even detect scents from over a mile away!

They use their powerful sense of smell to find food, track other animals, and sense danger. Coyotes also use smell to communicate with each other. They leave scent marks around their territory to let other coyotes know they live there. One sniff tells a coyote who was there, how long ago, and which direction they went.

A coyote's nose has over 200 million scent receptors. That is 40 times more than a human nose!

CLEVER CAMO

Dash! A coyote vanishes among the dry desert brush.

Coyotes have fur that helps them hide. Their coats are tan, brown, and gray. These colors match dirt, rocks, and dry grass.

The fur changes with the seasons. In summer, it looks more reddish-brown. In winter, it turns grayish to match snow and bare trees.

Coyotes crouch low when danger is near. They blend in so well that other animals might not see them.

Coyote pups are born with dark fur. Their coats get lighter as they grow.

CHOW
TIME

Chomp! The hungry coyote bites into a juicy melon.

Coyotes eat almost anything. They munch on rabbits, mice, and squirrels. They also eat birds, snakes, and insects.

Coyotes enjoy plants too. Fruits and berries are tasty treats. They love watermelons, apples, and peaches. They also eat grass and seeds.

A coyote eats about two to three pounds of food each day. In cities, they may also eat pet food or garbage. This varied diet helps them live anywhere.

Coyotes will even eat prickly cactus fruit in the desert.

CRAFTY HUNTERS

Coyotes can catch fish! They wade into shallow streams and grab them with their teeth.

Flick! A coyote's tail swings as it stalks through grass.

Coyotes are clever hunters. For small animals, they hunt alone using a special move called mousing. They listen carefully, then jump high in the air. They dive nose-first to catch prey hiding below.

Coyotes also stalk slowly and quietly through grass. Then they pounce quickly to grab their meal.

For bigger prey, coyotes work as a team instead. They take turns chasing deer until it gets tired. One coyote may chase while others wait ahead to help. This teamwork helps them catch food they could not get alone.

WATCH OUT

Crack! Dry twigs break. A coyote freezes and listens.

Coyotes must watch for big predators. Mountain lions hunt coyotes. Wolves hunt them too. They attack coyotes when they come into their territories.

Golden eagles swoop down from the sky to catch young pups. Great horned owls even hunt small coyotes at night.

In some places, alligators are a threat. Coyotes near water must stay alert.

Coyotes are smart enough to know when a wolf pack is nearby. They listen for howls and stay far away until the wolves move on.

QUICK GETAWAY

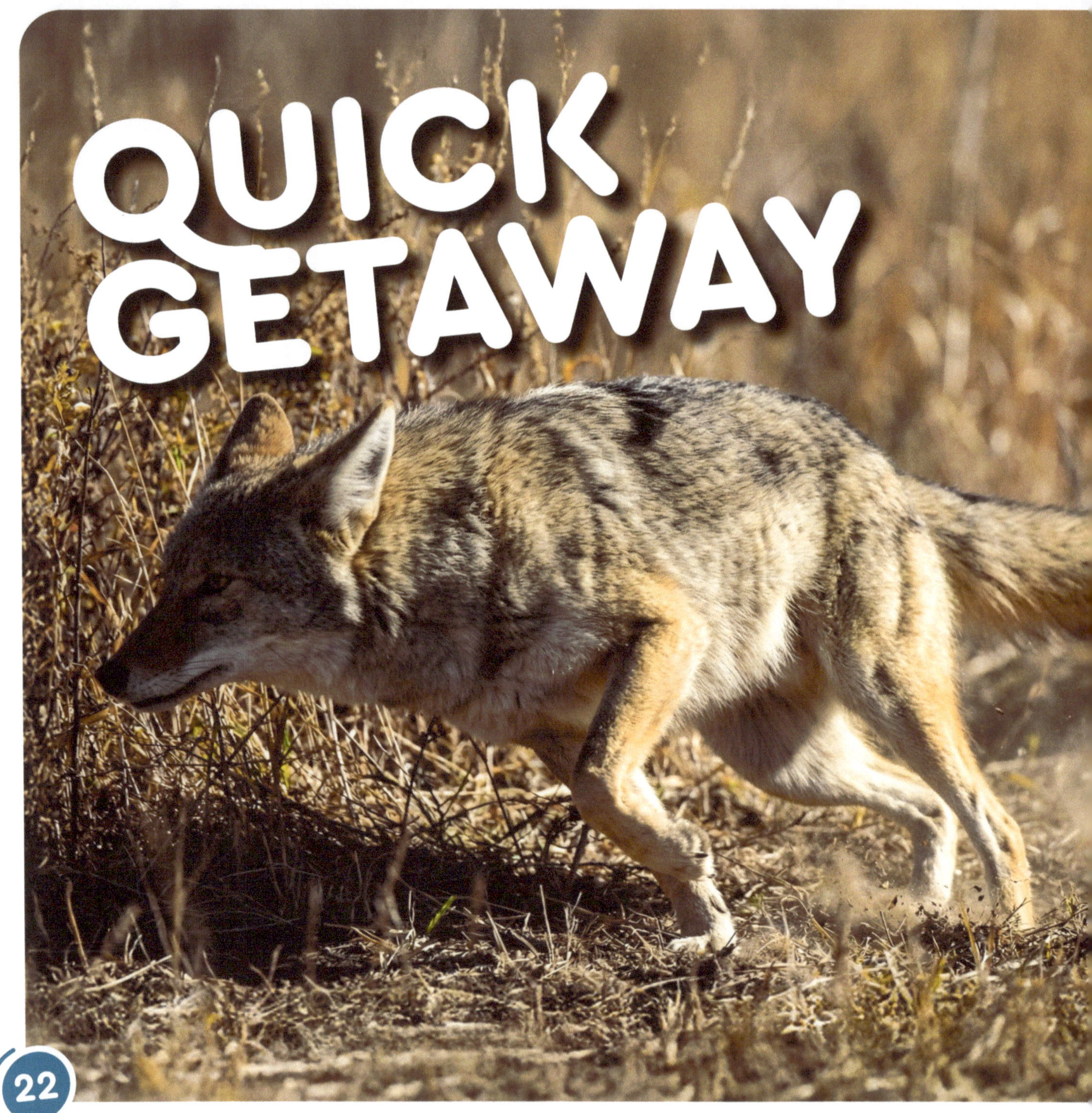

Sprint! A coyote runs into the bushes. It is gone in seconds.

Coyotes are fast runners. When a predator comes near, their first plan is to run away fast!

Sometimes running is not enough. Then hiding helps. Coyotes duck into thick brush. They hide in rocky dens. They crouch in tall grass to stay out of sight.

Coyotes use water to escape too. They swim across rivers. This helps them lose animals that chase them.

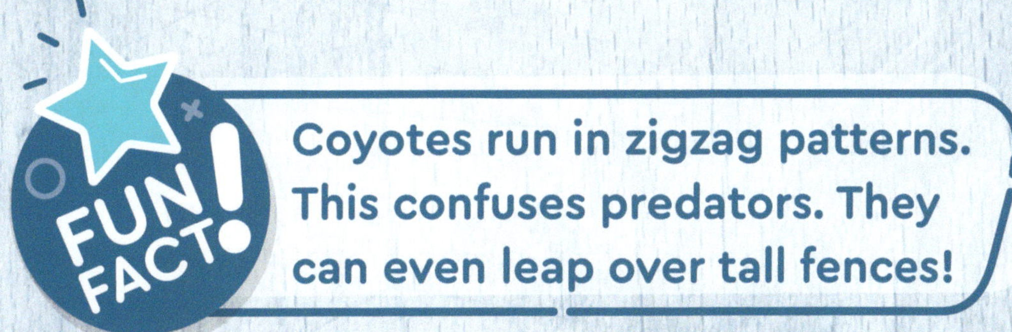

FAST FEET

Whoosh! A coyote races by in a blur of tan fur. It moves so fast!

Coyotes have long, thin legs built for speed. Their light bodies help them move fast. These features make coyotes great runners.

Coyotes can run up to 43 miles per hour in short bursts. That is faster than most dogs! They use this speed to get away from predators and also to catch prey.

Coyotes can also trot for many miles without getting tired.

Coyotes can swim at least half a mile across lakes and rivers. They paddle with all four legs!

DAY AND NIGHT

Yip, yip! The evening wind blows as coyotes begin to stir.

Coyotes are most active at dawn and dusk. These times are called **twilight**. The low light helps them hunt without being seen.

Coyotes rest during the hottest part of the day. They find shady spots to stay cool. This saves their energy for hunting later.

At night, coyotes roam and search for food. Their eyes have a special layer that helps them see in the dark.

Coyotes take short naps throughout the day instead of sleeping for many hours at once like humans do.

27

PACK LIFE

Snort! A coyote family meets at their cozy den.

Coyotes can live alone. They can also live in groups. A family group is called a pack. Packs have 3 to 7 members.

The mom and dad lead the pack. They are the alpha pair and they make all the big decisions, like where to hunt and when to move the den. The rest of the pack follows their lead. Older siblings help raise the new pups until they are old enough to go off on their own.

Coyote packs mark their land with urine and howls. This warns other coyotes to stay away.

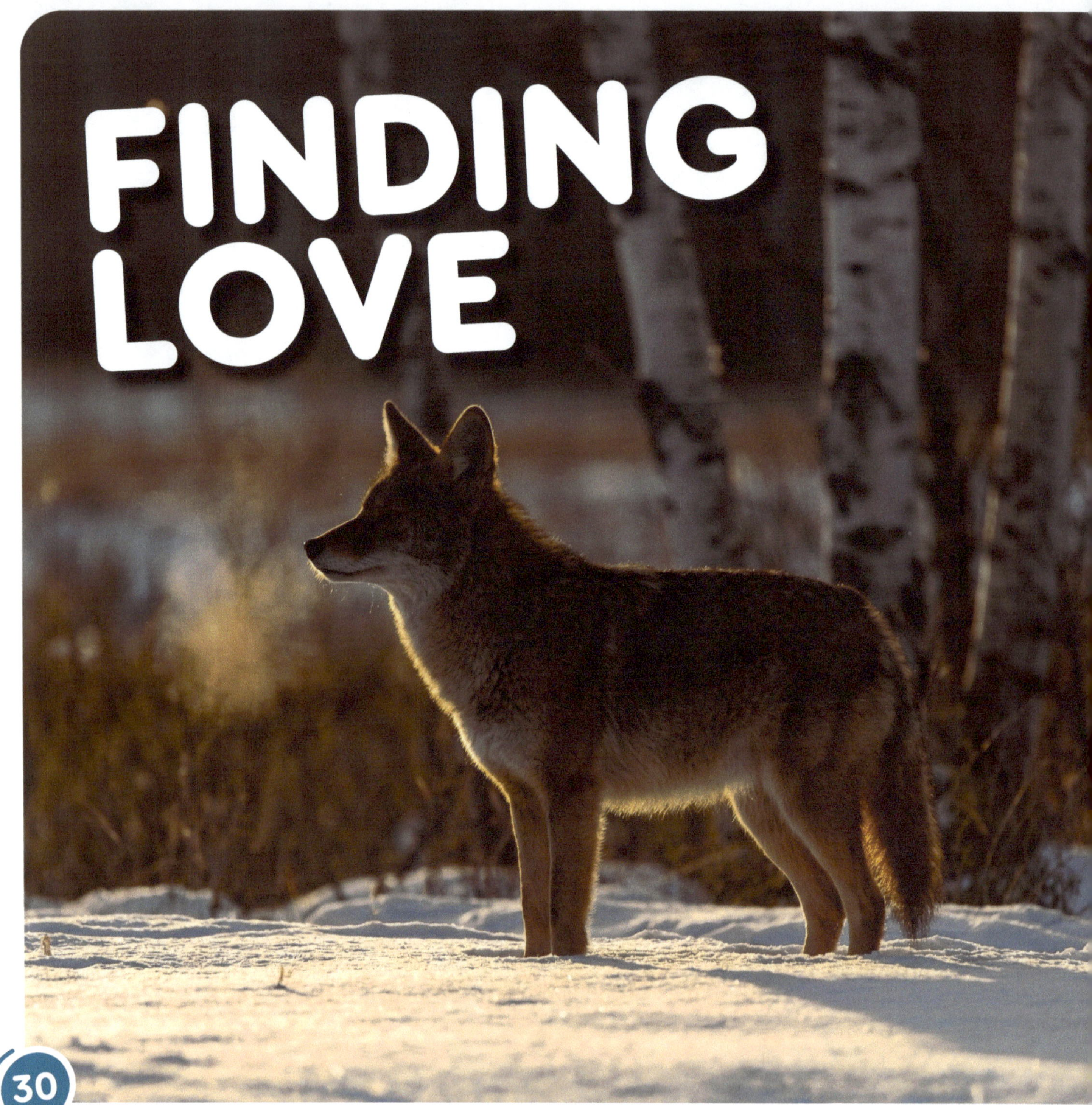

FINDING LOVE

Sniff! A male coyote sniffs the air. He's searching for his mate!

Coyotes mate once a year. This is in late winter. It happens from January to March.

Male coyotes howl to find females. They leave scent marks on rocks and trees. These scent marks help coyotes find each other.

A male and female may travel together for weeks. They hunt side by side, sleep near each other, and play together. This time helps them build a strong bond before their pups arrive in spring.

Coyote pairs often stay together for many years. Some mate for life. They raise pups together!

CUTE PUPS

DID YOU KNOW?
Coyote pups are born with blue eyes! They slowly change to the bright yellow-gold color that adult coyotes are known for.

Splash! Coyote pups tumble and play near a cool stream.

Baby coyotes are called pups. A mother coyote usually has a litter of four to seven pups. Some litters can have up to 19 pups!

Newborn pups are very small, weighing less than one pound. Their eyes are closed tight, and their ears are floppy and soft. They cannot see or hear for about two weeks.

Pups are born with short, dark brown or grayish fur. This fur turns yellow by the time pups are four months old. The pups stay safe in the den for about three to four weeks.

CARING COYOTES

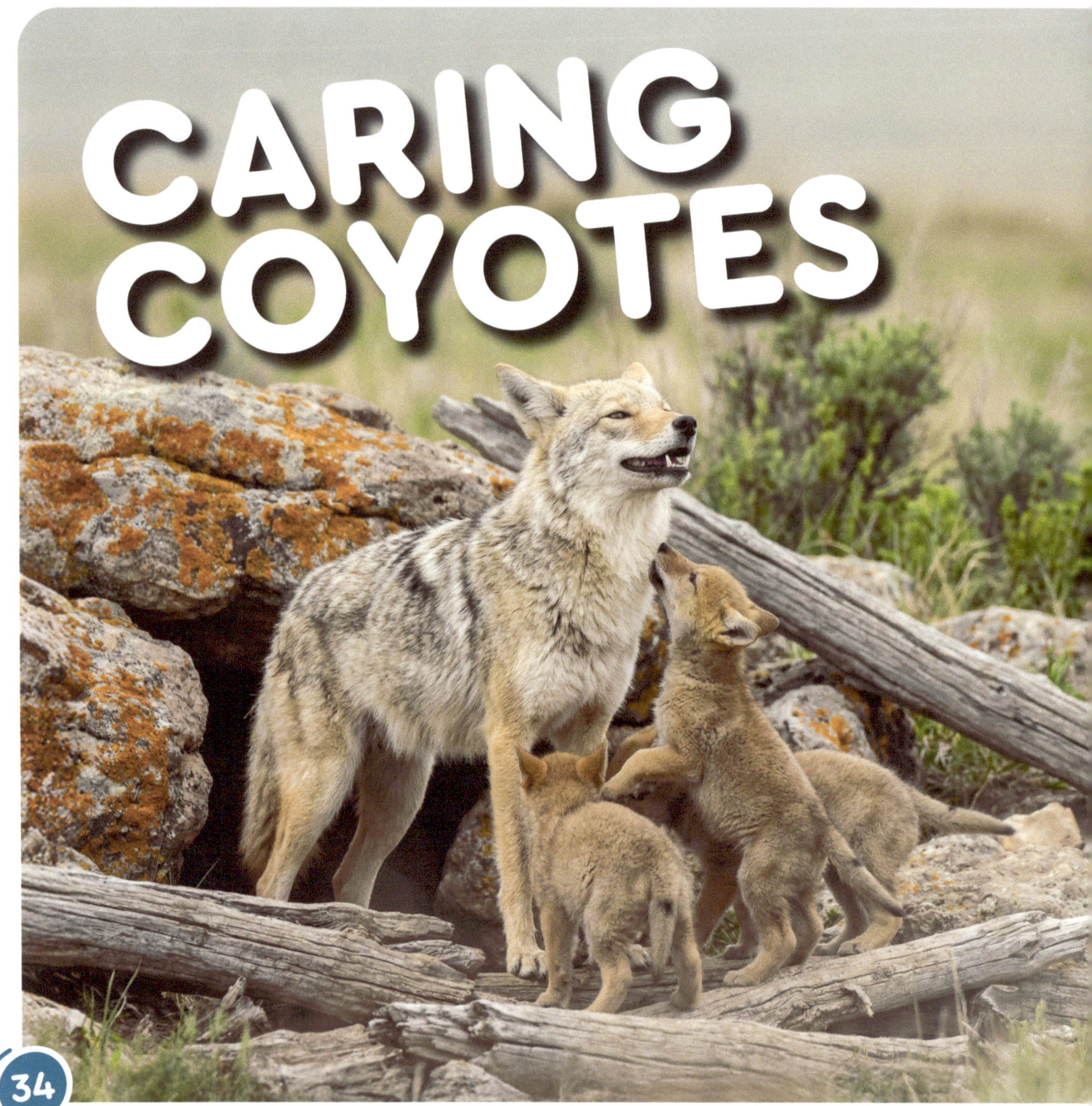

Jump! Young pups jump at their den entrance. They want to play!

Coyote parents work hard to raise their pups. Both the mother and father bring food to the den. They also protect the pups from danger.

Pups start eating solid food at about three weeks old. Parents chew meat and spit it up for the pups. This makes it easy for babies to eat.

Young coyotes learn to hunt by watching their parents. They practice pouncing on bugs and mice.

Older siblings often babysit the new pups while parents hunt.

SUPER
SURVIVORS

Look! A coyote trots through a city park at dawn.

Coyotes are super survivors. They have lived in North America for over one million years.

Many animals died out long ago. But coyotes kept going strong. Their secret is that they can change. When food is **scarce**, they eat whatever they can find. When their habitat is destroyed, they find a new one.

They are tough and smart.

Coyotes have been spotted living on top of parking garages, inside baseball stadiums, and even riding trains!

SPOT A COYOTE

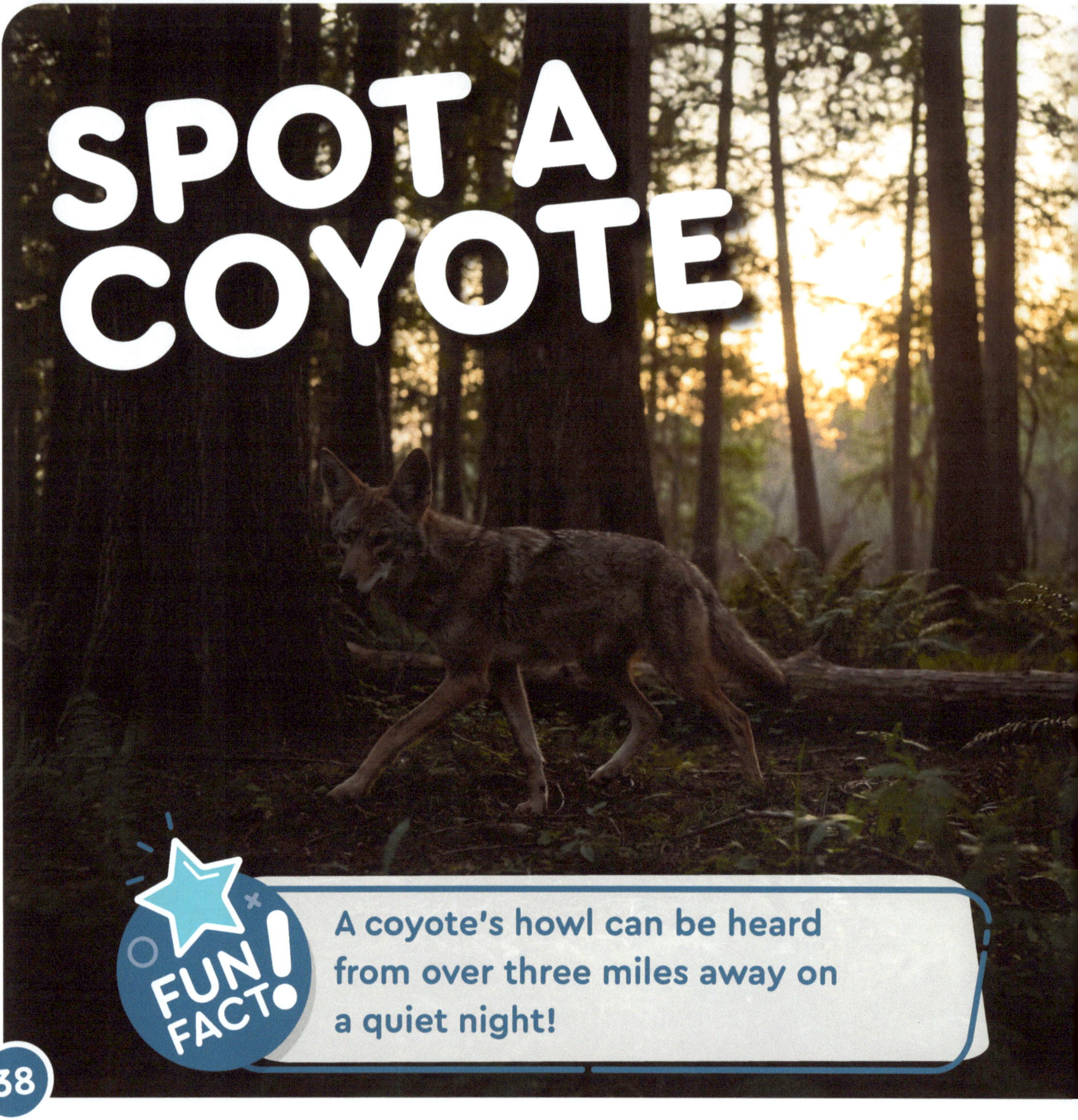

A coyote hears a human hiking at dusk. He changes paths to avoid being seen!

Coyotes are masters at hiding. Even if they live in your neighborhood, you might never see one! They are sneaky, quiet, and great at staying out of sight.

The best time to spot one is at dawn or dusk. Look in open fields, along trails, or at the edges of wooded areas. Bring binoculars so you can watch from far away.

If you cannot spot one, listen instead! Their howls carry for miles on quiet evenings. If you do see one, stay at least 100 feet away and never chase it. Just watch quietly and enjoy!

GLOSSARY

den
A cozy underground home where animals sleep and raise their babies.

prey
An animal that is hunted and eaten by another animal.

canine
The long, pointed teeth that animals use to grab and hold food.

scarce
Hard to find. When there is not much of something.

twilight
The time when the sky is partly light, just before sunrise or after sunset.